GENÈVE

ÉMIGRÉ

CHAO

Genève Chao is the child of émi-
grés, a translator of poetry between
French and English, and the author
of two other books of poetry. This
book is a monument to all the
strands of Chao's family.

ÉMIGRÉ
by Genève Chao
Copyright © 2018
All rights reserved
ISBN-13: 978-0-9987438-6-8

Tinfish Press is a 501(c)3 non-
profit, tax-exempt corporation
that supports the publication of
experimental poetry from the
Pacific. Tinfish books are available
from Small Press Distribution in
Berkeley, California (spdbooks.org)
and from our website.

TINFISH PRESS
Susan M. Schultz, Editor
47-728 Hui Kelu St. #9
Kāne'ohe, Hi. 96744
press.tinfish@gmail.com

Designed by Jeff Sanner

Support from the John Wythe
White & Victoria Gail-White's
Left Wing Right Brain Fund of the
Hawai'i Community Foundation
and individual donors.

www.tinfishpress.com

FOR THE SOUJOURNERS & FOR THE EVACUEES FOR THE SAILORS & FOR THEIR MEMORIES

This book is dedicated to the memory
of Margaret Maud Falla, née Le Cocq

Wish

every morning
into which you awaken
a straitjacket

chaque rêve
un déchaînement
furieux

tightens as if
a cocoon

A Primer

for a girl
child a book
containing tales
of babies dropped
down wells

un premier livre
instructif

a means
to erase
embarrassment

Avertissement

I never
promised you a
je ne t'ai rien
promis

je t'ai laissé
I left
you in drought

une sécheresse
absolue

this absence
this silence

Plainte

in this her
tiny voice
raised over
oceans

sa voix cries
faible falter
sous la under
fureur des waves'
vagues roar

Xanthie

on a small rock
in a wide sea

the light faded
the night came

a flutter of wings

you call it moth

I calls it night
butterfly, me

so the air
gentles

Mirage

durant des
over years
années après
after arrival

le voyage elle
she sought
regarda vers
on the

l'horizon

cherchant les
the hills
montagnes de
with her eyes

ses yeux
finding echoes
en trouvant
of land in
parfois dans
les nuages

clouds

Inheritance

he killed
all his children

qui aime
bien

for a better life

Wisp

Remants of
other tongues
remained in
her body

sometimes
leaping out
like foreign
ghosts

Spectre

to hâve
an outline
radieuse

a dazzlement
like reflets
or stars

circle and
flit a
cintre

all angles
and avarice

Aveu

il trouva
partout le
malheur

every hour
sounding
sorrow

a précision
blade turned
on itself

V'là qui vaout

too late desire
propelled him
to a pigsty

too late the lust
in handsful
of cress and rocket

scraps stolen
to batten

a stranger
on a rock

Mirror

to trace a
héritage an
inheritance to

descend as
a girl without
gravity

light skirts lighter limbs

ses yeux bridés pulled wide
in distant
innocence

Flleur

a practise of
waiting for
green points
& yellow flowers

bien plus longtemps
qu'auparavant

as if spring a
wave slowly
creeping from the east

the slowest
sunrise

là-bas des bouquets
of bunched trumpets
there déjà tout faits
readymade

Impact

they rolled the
canapés of
habit aside afin de
to make room
place for
other expressions
locales

Contain

in a cell a
crush of bodies
bondé de gens

flotsam and
lost on seas

in a port a
holding chamber
a hope for

privés de
light and air
creatures of
air et eau fraîche

in a hope an
issue,
forth

Prose

stiffening
for the necessary
lash

& mindful of
every moment
a failure

je tiens
toujours mes

to her waiting
eyes

lies, in a prayer
that this distant
heart still be

heard to you

Dé toutes la pus belle

the seconds before
waking into
strange sunlight a

dream of
a town crowning
hills a field of

dewspotted
daffs a room
with love on

every lip,
My love,
each saying a

swaddling

Hold

a boy in a room
draws letters on a wall
as a man in a room
scratches words in a wall

what speech for
what evidence
what grammar of
what dream

maisaon as refuge
hole as gaol

in both sentences
to wait

Half-tide

island to island
rock to rock a cell
grown out of crags

if you attends
at the patiemment
à la mi maraie tide
rising to your window

what light will block
what water will allow

à la mi-maraie the sun
came out un éclair
des ailes to light
on your rock like a bird

Averr

to wake
in the place
dreamed of

she walked
a mile and
another

crossed hills
to mountains
to have

fait un rêve
made a promise

over every
ridge the
absent coast

brutal et
absolu

Oimaïr

you could love
anything
that let you

a belief written in
tout port a berth of
reeds and rustles

un refrain to go
swinging scythes
under sun's roar

un chant, en
choeur, en canon

efforce yourself
to love
strange leaves
sticky tears

or, qu'all'oime
that she love
only roses

Ano'i

swinging scythes
under sun's soak
like sugar in water

a brow's sweat
streams the same
on any island

cane or wheat
corn or coffee

he keeps head down
and back round

in soft weather
dreams of
hard winds

Creitre

for Lilit

a flower
a root
take hold
on certain
soil,

each tendril
a push
through foreign
earth

géranium ou
marguerite,
a child une
fille qui fait
des bonds d'tchu

seeking the
à la recherche
d'une salt of
terre connue
home

rolled head
over feet in
new grass

Embed

after a
space of years a
shape pressed
in the mattress

softens
shells
to shed

a memory of
heavy sleep des
rêves inespérés
unhoped-for

so tender
skin when
sudden
suspicion

habit
hardens habitude
to coutûme
our custom

bleu
bruise

Moi

mon prince
sourd et
impassible

sovereigns
in grass or
gold

figures
of dream or
nightmare

unblinking
to a cry

Brulaïr

in flickers
a faraway
field burns

une incendie
lointaine et
silencieuse

as the green
kō in smoke
smudged
skies

the news an
ashen country
strewn with
cold hands

le retour to
black clouds
blank earth

Assaïz

the sky
exploded
again

enough to
shake our
shaky ground

en flammes
a fiery
souvenir d'une
of
vie antérieure
life

a flicker a
memory
trembling

Monument

A plot of
listing stones
bowed with
years

a gran'mère
older than
walls watching

un océan
whose rumble dulls
homely voices

a man
qui can
réfuse water
from that sweet
source

R'vins

in each
return a
reflet

of foregone
selves, des photos
superposed

je me l
find where
memory is

and seek you
recherche
among our dead
perdu

Lune

every brusque
matin sonne
the bells for   blank burning
bossing   brown brows

we signed   in the minutes
un contrat   before réveil
our years in   l'espoir une
échange   bubble rising

howling lunas   in your gorge,
faces blanches   son impossible
                               évanescence

Seraïe

dans ton
in your
cœur une
heart a
flamme

brûlant
for home
place pour
le pays natal
burning

dans la
evening
soirée
un vent
qui risque
wind

might to
le moucher
snuff it

Viar

for R.G.F.

I will
je voudrais
stop forever
and not go
ever rester
en vie die
back

à jamais
if only to
si seulement
to see the
pour voir
passer les
ships home,
me

Tombeau

another of
le cœur brisé
another of
une solitude
another of
la distance
a cancer
a canker

l'aoute et
l'autre qui
succombe sans
souffle with
stones less
breath

in lines like
bons écoliers
sunflowers
to attend a
master's hand

Comme
de raisaon

and yet
each spring
shoot forth dear
leaves

this belle
saison notre
content swell
with
secrets

to burst a
salient bud
shows love or
magic

comme de
raisaon of course
it comes
alors from
us

Rain

we were two
bits of a rock
broke off

un bout de
home cast à
vau l'eau in
strange waters

to hew in
your dark current
to cleave
in that cold stream

when you
left you took
tu m'arraches
la pllie the sky
des cieux
with you

Kōpaʻa

every bend
of back a
crack a
dance

tu fais
dos rond
comme si
de rien n'était

you disappear
in rows of
identical
spines
le même
effort le même
chagrin in same
strain in same
sorrow

Travas

when in the light
un chant de
of each morning

the same day come
hirondelle un oiseau de
the work be done

inhalation
nuit les secrets qu'on
a resolve to

s'y consacrer
une dédicace

we awoke and
délices de
decided there's

no place for day
ne pas se déplier
but in sleeping

tight buds or
sealed letters

Weft

when
the string
that held her
to it snapped

at last
quand

enfin
se cassa
la corde qui
la nourissait

Hua

from dark
germ and soaked
soil une attente

for weight of
une vigne chargée
full fruit to drop

une mappemonde pops
in his mouth sweet
and round

his work a patience
une fuite incant
the sweeter season

Djère

they went out
in the last boat

moppets with
poupées and

frogs in their
pockets ils
revinrent

no longer
habitants

de cette
small île

l'Iliet

of day wrenched
to le laisser défait
leave unmade as

le to trust rooms
droit de keep our place
retour over oceans

if patient l'impression
d'un corps body still
pressed there

we only meant à
peine lâché
to leave a moment

we left our pillow
still dented nous avons
cru pouvoir r'venir

a book's slot
fills quick cédé
once lost

Riocque

for Gerard

we loved not
to solve problems
or win wars

pousse une fleur
délicate être à fleur
de toute peau

love a luxury
shines
on a pillow

doux et
inutile et
pourtant

what better use
could I put to
than you

Hoku

with winds
comme des
through channels
fourmis on
sifting sand
grimpe les uns
into glass, every
sur les autres
chamber packed
se hissent
tight with bodies
jusqu'aux toits
in boxes in alleys
afin de voir
finally to climb
enfin la lueur
to see stars
des étoiles

Appeule

we decide une
it won't smart
to turn to danse de
silhouettes absences
on dock or une
deck disparition

we watch regarde la
as bodies become lente
dolls and dolls douleur
dots a call de toi qui
held silent in me
our throats quittes

there are j'aurais
always other préféré
methods le cri qui
I could have attend
waited until ce sang
you slept to assourdi
disappear

Saeure

mark the
days
une date
barrée
until we
may be
conter les
jours
back in
this
jusqu'au
retour

Ente

there
ci et là
a hope to
faire pousser
grow like
l'espoir
seeds une
germe qui
cleave la
pierre
dare not
whisper

Vièdjer

in a handful
petit son petit
of sweets all
monde si doux
needed pleasures

or in horizons
grand son grand
of ocean all
manque si douloureux
emptied joy

Fôim

days into
enfin
nights of
la faim
labour
gagne

nights
affamés
into days
de tout
of hunger
poison

Rabat'e

he turns regarde
to look bien ce
back until pays en
land grows dispar-
distant ition

puis il no more
se dresse I go
vers un walking
horizon this soft
lointain ground

Baillier

in circle this
geste perdu
dance our   the old dance
une esquisse   un deuil les
lost labours   to mourn
un souvenir   jeunes par
sunrise on   the young as
un ici fixe   respect une
abandoned   obeisance
lands   révérence
                             our past now
                             passée en
                             a present

Hele loa

to go with
partir à ne
no hope of
jamais revenir
returning

puis habiter
hope shameless
l'espoir sans
and intent to
honte at last

to home

55

Afterword

This book was written in Los Angeles in 2017, a year in which the political regime new to power waged a more explicit cultural and legislative war on immigrants than this century could have imagined and in which those of us who had lived in a United States that claimed to celebrate our many origins came abruptly and rudely to the realisation that we were not, in fact, as welcome as we had believed;

the word 'immigrant' is someone who comes into a place, of course, and (in our English) its converse, 'emigrant,' is less used, calling attention as it does to the place of origin, the lost home, the history of families and migrations. An immigrant is an incrusté, an interloper, whereas an emigrant is someone who has gone out. An émigré is thus one who is absent from the place that was once home. We forget, even those of us in the process of so doing, that immigration is not merely a process of glomming onto a place like barnacles on the hull of a boat, but is a process of transplantation in which parts of an organism are necessarily damaged or lost; emigration is almost always preceded by exigency, waves of emigration more so. The people of Guernsey know this; during the second World War their Island, strategically located in the English Channel, overlooking the whole of the continent of Europe, was occupied by Nazi forces and the vast majority of children were evacuated to England, Scotland, or Wales. These children were separated from their families for five years, often returning with a manner of speech unfamiliar to their families, whose faces might, in turn, be unfamiliar to them;

a connection might be drawn between this severing of the attachment to "home" and that of the soujourner workers who emigrated from China to Hawai'i in the late 19th and early 20th centuries, there to endure demeaning working conditions and inexorable loneliness. To emigrate is isolating, not because it necessarily cuts us off from human contact but because it removes us from our human contexts;

there is a way of being that is home and that cannot be replicated once removed over oceans. There are words that fall away or morph into new ways of expression, as Hawaiian morphs into pidgin, as Norman French becomes the 'patois' so few Guerns now remember, but which was a feature of life there before the war;

this book is an effort at remembering. In the fall of 2016 I was speaking to Margaret Falla, a former evacuee and émigrée from Guernsey, in her home in America, a home where decades earlier she had offered to teach the child me to crochet (I declined) and instructed me on the proper way to fold sheets (I listened). She told me then that

she missed Guernsey fiercely, and I conceived a desire to bring her home one last time;

this desire was not to be realised in life. She died in America as my Chinese grandfather died in America, an ocean away from home –

in this book are preserved some of the languages of this emigrant history and some of the laments that were so long kept quiet, out of deference to those of us who came after and the new home we hope we have made.

TINFISH

ALSO AVAILABLE FROM
TINFISH PRESS:

Leona Chen, *Book of Cord*, 2017

Shiro Murano, Translated by Goro Takano, *On Lost Sheep*, 2017

Yu Xinqiao, Edited and Translated by Yunte Huang, *The Last Lyric*, 2017

Timothy Dyke, *Atoms of Muses*, 2017

Liang Yujing, *Zero Distance*, 2017

Wawa, *Pei Pei the monkey king*, 2016

Kaia Sand, *A Tale of Magicians Who Puffed Up Money that Lost its Puff*, 2016

Lissa Wolsak, *Of Beings Alone: The Eigenface*, 2016

Jonathan Stalling, *Lost Wax: Translation Through the Void*, 2015

Albert Saijo, *WOODRAT FLAT*, 2015

Norman Fischer, *Escape This Crazy Life of Tears* (Japan, July 2010), 2014

Donovan Kūhiō Colleps, *Proposed Additions*, 2014

Lehua M. Taitano, *A Bell Made of Stones*, 2013

Steve Shrader, *The Arc of the Day |
The Imperfectionist*, 2013

J. Vera Lee, *Diary of Use*, 2013

Jack London is Dead: Contemporary Euro-American Poetry in Hawai'i (and Some Stories),
edited by Susan M. Schultz, 2012

Ya-Wen Ho, *last edited [insert time here]*, 2012

Maged Zaher, *The Revolution Happened and You Didn't Call Me*, 2012

Jai Arun Ravine, แล้ว *and then entwine*, 2011

Elizabeth Soto, *Eulogies*, 2010

Kaia Sand, *Remember to Wave*, 2010

Daniel Tiffany, *The Dandelion Clock*, 2010

Paul Naylor, *Jammed Transmission*, 2009

Lee A. Tonouchi, *Living Pidgin: Contemplations on Pidgin Culture*,
2nd edition, 2009

Lisa Linn Kanae, *Sista Tongue*, 2nd edition, 2008

Craig Santos Perez, *from unincorporated territory [hacha]*, 2008 [out of print]

Meg Withers, *A Communion of Saints*, 2008

Hazel Smith, *The Erotics of Geography*, 2007

Linh Dinh, *All Around What Empties Out*, 2003, [out of print].
Subpress/Tinfish

Caroline Sinavaiana-Gabbard, *Alchemies of
Distance*. 2001, [out of print]. Subpress/
Tinfish/Institute of Pacific Studies

For other TinFish Press publications, including chapbooks and *TinFish* journals
1-20, visit our website: tinfishpress.com or order from spdbooks.org.

When I circle all the words I do not know in Chao's *Émigré*, the pages become bold with textual mime. Thought bubble after thought bubble of bl-understanding test one's openness to learning. Chao's powerful work obliges us as, more than readers, social actors in a very real world. Again and again, the poems ask us – in regret, in defiance, in hope – if we can be as curious, patient, and kind towards human beings as words. I dare you to rise to the challenge.

–Ya-Wen Ho

émigré, in its interweaving of four languages, is a strange experiment for the reader, as if their own language were delocalized, moving into and out of tongues as one follows the continuum of the text. And the tour de force is probably that the speech, in these poems, seems to take place in an unlocated interval – a space in between, "like foreign / ghosts."

–Alain Cressan

A slip, a lilt, doucement into the folds of this book, and there you will find "a précision/blade turned" -- in these delicate, sharply turning moments of near-translation, my mind's ear flickers back and forth, no terre to land upon, no land to rester en place. I sit beside the restless murmur of Genève Chao's language, the echoes of nouns and verbs that refuse domestication, resist the erasure – of those who have left, *émigré*, wondering, "brutal/ et absolu."

–Sawako Nakayasu